MIND NOISE

By

Ash Raymond James

#	Title
11	HELLO
14	GET UP
15	GETTING OLD
18	PERFECT P1
28	200 POUNDS
30	LOVEHARD CAFE
33	MOTHER BIRD
34	WINTER
41	SAILOR
42	OPPOSABLE
46	EXTRA HOUR
50	BROTHER
61	LTB PT 1
65	FALSE ALARM
68	AUTISM
72	SOLO

20	22	25	26
PERFECT P2	RAW	HOPE	BLACK CAT 13

36	37	38	40
CHORUS	SCHEME	STATIC	AVALANCHE

53	54	56	59
COLOURS	ODE TO TONY	MINDFRUIT	ROGUE ALLURE

73	74	76	77
BLACK AND YELLOW	SNOW	DRIVE	SOS

78 TEXAS	**80** LTB PT 2	**84** BOX	**85** OPINIONS
97 TAXIMAN	**102** ROLLER-COASTERS	**105** AUTHENTIC	**106** UNBORN
114 STILLNESS	**116** THE CLASSIC	**120** LTB PT 3	**123** SELF LOVE
			132 WISILY PT 3

87 FARE
88 WISILY PT 1
89 FEATHERS
92 BONE SHAKER

109 THE ROAD
110 THE AGE
112 WISILY 2
113 1ST KISS

124 RAINBOW
126 WEATHERED
128 LOVE DRUNK
130 MINUS LIFE

135 THE FANTASM FACTORY

2020 Ash Raymond James

All rights reserved

ISBN: 9798650615545

INTRODUCTION

The term 'mind noise' stemmed from a poem I wrote a few years ago. It is a term I have used ever since to describe the madness in my mind. The never-ending thoughts, the poems, the stories, the designs, the ideas etc. That poem is the first one you will read as nothing else could start this book better than that poem. This book is a gallery of all the things that contribute to that noise. This book is a gathering of pieces I have written over the years in a number of different places and stages of my life and I am proud of the final outcome. I wrote this book but in no way is this book mine. For every one of you who relates to anything in here, a piece of that poem in now yours. For anybody who felt a damn thing from any of these poems, the same applies to you. I hope through my experiences, it helps shed some light on your own. This book is for the lovers. This book is for the fighters. This book is for everybody drowning in the static of their mind noise.

Always to Savvy

There is so much
mind noise,
I hear the demons
stomping down
my mind stairs
onto my mind beach,
pitchforks in hand
destroying
my mind peace.
I have lost my mind.

xx———

Hi/I'm not good at first impressions/I'm a second or
third sort of guy/imagine you're adjusting your TV
sets/we're going to get the clear picture eventually.

Let's begin. Hello//my name is Ash and I'm at war
with my mind noise! By mind noise, I mean/brain static
and by brain static I mean this
demolition derby inside my head. Hope and Doubt/
rev their engines/floor it and prepare for impact//
may the best man win.

Let's begin. Hi//my name is Bear and I'm a
rambling woodland in need of more adventure.
Too long away from the wild and the melody of joy
slowly begins to disintegrate inside me and I stop
humming the tune of sunrise.

Let's begin. Greetings//My name is Ashy//
I'm an old romantic who laughs at his own jokes//
and I am a magnet to sadness. I'm all for distant sounds.
The whistle of a train a few miles away and thunder a
few cities over. I love rain anywhere
though. Tin roof or collision with skin

Let's begin. Howdy partner//My name is
Ashtronaut//I'm a little bit out of this world/and/out
of my mind. I spend most nights perched on the edge of
my spaceship fishing for shooting stars.

Let's begin. Hey//My name is Ash Raymond James
and if you have the time, I'd like to share a few things.
So, tell me, are you ready? Well then....

HELLO

PLAY ▶

00:00:00

RAW

Hi, I'm Ash,
Not really though
my name is Ashley
but I've never liked that name.
I'm 28 young going on 28 old,
I'm six-foot-tall on my good days
and I don't like pineapple on my pizza.
I also know today is Tuesday
and I probably deserve a medal
for knowing that, let me explain why.
Some days, I barely make it
as far as the light switch,
I sometimes close the curtains for days,
turn off my phone
and disappear into
the dark side of my mind.
See I suffer from a bunch of letters.
There's ASD, ADHD, OCD
and just D.
D is for depression.
D is for don't get out of bed.
D is for don't go outside.
D is for don't shower, don't eat
and whatever you do, don't breathe.
D is for don't you dare believe in yourself.
D is for drugs. D is for drink.

15

I just want to feel something
I just want to feel nothing
I just want to be somebody else,
I just want to be more than a mannequin
in a shop window
for mental health awareness
and outrun the cliques
but I'm just not that quick.
I've been sober for nearly four years now
but D is still for drowning.
I drown in my temptations,
I just want something to take
the edge off
before I take off the edge...
On the worst of days,
D, is for die
it's on loop in my head
the edge off
before I take off the edge...
On the worst of days,
D, is for die
it's on loop in my head
like some catchy radio jingle
that no matter how much

I ignore,
I know I'll eventually
start singing
but not today...
because today
is Tuesday
and today,
D ,
D is for don't give up
D is for don't worry
because today
I believe it is going
to be
okay.

Get up.
Even if you
feel like the anchor
on the seabed,
get up.

The skies
sent the rain
to knock on your window
to ask if you
wanted to come outside
and play.
The sun ray ninjas
crept in
to dance on your skin
and didn't you notice?
It was their
'hey, fancy a little date
with fresh air' dance.

So, get up.
The world
is calling you
and it would be rude
not to answer.

G
E
T

U
P

PERFECT

PART 1

I think it's about time we notice
that flaws are our forte.
Mistake is just a synonym
for lesson
and perfection is a seed
planted by somebody
with too much ego.

Perfection is the pipe dream.
We have all said
the wrong thing at the wrong time
and bathed in self hatred.
We have all hurt somebody
whether it was intentional
or not.

We all know the lyrics
to that song titled:
Sorry, I messed up.
We have all got lost
in mirrors trying to recognise
who's staring back.

We, are all
riddled with mountains
of mistakes
and it's about time
we notice,
this
is what makes us
human.

PERFECT

PART 2

Okay,
there is a difference
between being perfect
and being perfect
for somebody.

When I met her
our mistakes
mingled like Tetris
and mistake after mistake,
the weight that they carried
simply disappeared.
Those mountains
became molehills
and every piece of her
lined up perfectly
with every piece of me.
Her imperfections
wore a sundress,
spruced up its hair
and made me say
dumb things like
'hot damn'.

Her imperfections
know how to shake it
to show me
their good intentions.

She is far from perfect
but quite honestly,
I wouldn't
want her
any other way.

GETTING OLD

Today,
I have a support bandage
on my wrist
and there is no incident
to report.
There's no pinpoint trigger,
no funny story
only my body deciding
it no longer
wants these parts to work.

My body has grown too old
for maintenance.
It has become the old dude
trying to use the latest tech.
My body still runs on Windows 95
and my memories
are stored on floppy disks.

When I wake up these days
I creak like a haunted house
and even my ghosts
have grown lazy
but I don't care.

Body, this is a letter to you.
You can slow down,
you can take a day off
from your scheduled repairs
and you can bring on
the aching and
the random bruising.
You can put my strength
to sleep but listen
and listen good.
No matter how much
you try to convince me
I'm not able,
however much
you try to tell me
I can't,
I will always find a way
to prove you wrong.
Body, you can scream in pain
and make my bones
go on strike
but there is no protest
powerful enough

to stop this train from running.
Body, let me sign this letter
with a middle finger
because even on your best day
you will never
strip me of my youth.

It's the sun squeezing through the crack
in the blinds.
It's the flickering streetlight
refusing to quit.
It's the memory box
that survived the flood
in the basement.
It's every morning you wake up.
It's every day you survive through.
It's every night you manage to sleep.
Hope, it's all around you.
Hope, it's inside you.

H
O
P
E

BLACK CAT 13

I was raised superstitious.
The playground became a land mine
and all things innocent grew claws
and learnt how to roar.
I became so cautious, it was dangerous.
The monster under my bed
was a broken mirror
and doomsday was always
on the horizon
labelled Friday the 13th.
I would collect pennies
like I was a survivor
on a desert island
on the verge of starvation,
I learnt how to ration luck.
Then, 28 years of pennies later
I met her and nowadays,
I would ballet under a thousand ladders,
I would moonwalk over the cracks
of side walks in a million cities
and leap over an army
of black cats in my path.
I would poke holes in the ceiling,
pop open an umbrella
and dance on a blanket

of poured salt
whilst performing
singing in the rain.
I will flip the bird
to every magpie
in passing
because as long as I
get to call her mine,
isn't it obvious?
That is all the luck,
I will ever need.

200 POUNDS

I am 200 pounds of fidget.
I am pure bred frantic and fuss.
I am a vhs cassette
constantly trying
to shake the dust
off my jacket,
and by jacket I mean skin
and by dust, I mean existence.
I have rewound myself so much
I am scratches and static,
I am anything but still.
My mind is an instant replay
of old hallways
and every basement ever.
I move to dodge the memories,
I'm loud to drown out the thoughts,
I dance to the sound of distraction
and I am afraid of silence.

There are days I am the sort of tired
where I feel it beyond my bones.
I become a puppet
where my strings are pulled
by some part of me
refusing to quit,
still desperate to dodge the scissors.
I am 200 pounds of mountain crawl,
and even lifeless I'm in motion;
my body trying to outrun my mind,
and I don't think there's anything
that will ever slow me down.

LOVE HARD CAFE

Love as a teenager
is pretty much anybody
who is willing to have sex with you.
Love in college, is the girl who sits
at your table because she says
you look lonely.
Love at eighteen is like
a religion you've lost faith in
yet you still pray to from time to time.
Love at twenty-five
is the first girl at the bar
after you've just realised
you're twenty-five
and you're running out of
time to settle down.
Love is the sport
you stopped playing
due to injury
yet you still try to run the field
occasionally
despite the doctors orders.
Love on the dark days

is a smile from a stranger
that your brain translates to,
she's the one,
we're going to get married,
we're going to have three kids,
we're going to move out
to the country
and live a simple life
but deep down,
you know love is that feeling
you haven't felt yet.
Love is the hole inside you that you try
so desperately to fill
with all the wrong things.
Love looks a whole lot like
loneliness sometimes
but that's a completely different
black-hole inside of you.
Sure, kindness has sounded like wedding bells
but if you listen closer,
you'll see it's just your heart
finding its rhythm again.

Love is the blank canvases
I have covered with ideals
yet I don't really know
what I should be painting.
Love, I don't know
what your face looks like,
I don't know what coffee shop
you hide in
to read your books and
slip an extra sugar in your tea
but believe me,
I will never stop looking for you
and I promise, some day soon,
I am going to find you.

Let us celebrate
with empty shoulders
and helium hearts.
Let us be nothing
but free
even if it's only
for this collection
of moments.
Let us celebrate
your campfire heart
warming all those
lost in the haze
of their own winter.
Let us celebrate
your lighthouse spirit,
the endless welcoming
to all of those lucky enough
to follow your light
and find you.
Let us celebrate you,
every fragment
and every atom.
It is the least
you deserve

MOTHER

BIRD

WINTER

There's no winter better
than the winter that dances
where summer should be.
That winter doesn't care
about your plans,
that winter doesn't listen
to your dreams
or anticipations,
that winter doesn't give a fuck.
That winter was the winter
where we stood in snow
under cloud coverage
where sun rays
should have been
and you told me
the best things in life
come unexpected.
You explained to me
that like this winter
we can be where we want to be
when we want to be there.
You taught me that we can drown
in our sadness
or we can learn to swim.

We can make the best of a bad situation
or we can wallow in it.
We can go home,
we can take off the wet gloves,
we can crawl into bed
and wait for the sun to return
or we can say fuck you
right back!
This winter,
was a lot of things
but thanks to you,
I never let it be
victorious.

CHORUS

I have been darkness
for most my life.
Light merely a distant thing.
Then there was you,
always shaking off
the sun sparkles
even in winter.

You were the torch giver,
the bringer of flames,
and you made sunlight
out of kind words
and gentle touches
from your finger brushes.

The beauty
was always there
but now,
thanks to you,
it sings.

I'm a static addict
lost in the havoc
of my madness.
My mind
is a woodland cabin
on another planet.
I'm a magnet
to manic sadness,
pulled into my panic palace.
I'm a battered artist
always pedalling backwards
into the unsettling vastness
of my deafening darkness.
Even my hope is heartless,
my faith departed,
fresh starts disregarded,
I'm too far gone
to clean the canvas,
so off I fade
home again
back into blackness.

.

SCHEME

'If I can silence this static, beautiful poetry will surely flourish.'

AN AVALANCHE IS JUST NATURES WAY OF SAYING 'GOD DAMMIT, I'M DONE!' AND TODAY AVALANCHE, I FEEL YOU BRO.

I have outgrown sadness.
I am beyond that definition,
I am something
I cannot explain.

Imagine a sailor
lost at sea
who spots a lighthouse
yet his ship
refuses to steer,

I would know
of his struggles.

S
A
I
L
O
R

OPPOSABLE

If cats had thumbs,
I'm 99% sure they'd rule the world.
Cats don't need to talk,
they're already purrsuasive
and if you look deep enough
into their eyes,
you can see they're just waiting
for evolution to kick in.

If cats had thumbs
we'd have people like
Cat the ripper
and Harold Nipman
and the hiss-tory books
would be cluttered
with tails of cleocatra
and ruthless Furers
and it would be
a cat-astrophe.

If cats had thumbs
they'd rebuild amphitheaters
and bring back gladiators

and all the blood sports
and give thumbs downs
constantly
because all cats find
a-mews-ment in murder and
watching the world burn.

Cats are the answer
to the question,
how will the world end?
And there is evidence.

Cats will lay on your face
and try to suffocate you.
Cats will lick themselves
in.... places
then lick your face.
Cats will beg
for your attention
by headbutting you
then when they're
done with your attention
they will rip apart
your skin with their claws.

If there was a cat equivalent
of Christmas,
we'd have Santa claws
who'd sneak into your house
shit under your tree,
destroy your couch,
watch you clean up the mess
and then demand dinner.

Cats never get stuck in trees,
they just climb them
so the firemen
can't attend real emergencies!

Listen,
cats are evil
So believe me now
or regret it fur-ever.

Let's make love
with the
intensity
of a million
dying stars
at lightspeed.

EXTRA HOUR

It's Thursday and it's eleven
which means I'm here again.
In the same waiting room
watching the same paint
fall off the walls,
it's as desperate to leave as me.
The same receptionist
gives me the same form
whilst she completes a crossword
from the same magazine
using the same pen, it's just routine.
We sit on chairs
just because they're chairs
but occasionally I sit on tables
just to feel out of sync.
Routine is my comfort zone in
chaos
but the rules still unsettle me
sometimes.
Anyway, it's been
nine hours and
I'm still a ghost.

I still feel nothing.
I spent half hour last week
talking about dinosaurs
which cost me a weeks worth of
lunch,
but they tell me it'll get better,
my friends say I seem happier
and I guess that's good.
I don't feel it, I still feel like me
which is the person I'm trying to
escape.
I still stare at the sky and fail to feel
hope.
I just see disaster.
Sometimes I pray for asteroids
just so I can be gone and it
wouldn't be my fault.
She tells me that's depression,
she once used spectacular and
suicide
in the same sentence
and that still makes me
feel unsettled
 yet I still come back here.

48

She told me that's a sign
that I believe in something
but really I just don't want to
drive in the city
and she has a voice I can tolerate.
Plus she only has six things
about her that annoy me
which is a record.
We talk for an hour about things
that don't seem relevant but
apparently they are.
I always end it
with the same question,
to which she always responds yes,
we just need more time,
we're making progress
but without me can she afford the
haircut?
My problems are her financial solution
and that leaves me unsettled.
If we all had our shit together
she'd be working minimum wage
clutching faux leather...

I don't know,
it just leaves me unsettled.
However, I still look at her
and ask, hey,
if we had an extra hour
could you bring me back to life?

BROTHER

If I have ever called you brother
then you best grab your coat
because I'm bringing the storms to you.
If I've ever called you brother
please understand that I'm sorry.
When I say brother,
what I'm really saying is thank you.
I see a life line in you.
You are the voice of reason,
you are the rescue cushion
before the splat,
you save me before I know
I need saving.
Just know, if I have ever
called you brother
your battles become my battles.
I will stand on the front line,
I will take the first bullet,
I will camp for days on a rooftop,

I will take the last bullet
but I will never let you fight alone.
If I have ever called you brother,
it means I love you
and you can bet your bottom dollar
that I always god damn will.

We are
the sinners
and the saviours
and none of us
are clean slated

Painted
a thousand shades
of ache
on battered canvas.
Haunted
by the hues
of uncertainty.
There is old paint
under the new,
a reminder
 that this isn't an eternity,
this is only the now.

COLOURS

ODE TO TONY

Tony introduced himself to me,
the way only Tony knew how.
By wrapping a pool cue
around my skull
and then justifying it
using the phrase
'well, you know how it is'.
Tony doesn't like losing.
Tony is constantly on edge,
scratch that, Tony is the type of guy
who's like the cartoon
who's just plunged over the cliff
miraculously suspended
in mid air defying all scientific beliefs.
Tony is the kind of guy
who grows a third arm in a bar fight.
Tony speaks two languages
English, barely.
Fisticuffs in a dark alleyway, fluently.
Tony taught me how to land a punch,
Tony piloted me through
the darkest parts of my life.

He was the only one brave enough to
rip the drink from my hands
and tell me I've had too much.
He was the only man
who had enough strength
to drag me back home
after twelve pints of self pity.
Yes, Tony has a criminal record
and his living room is practically on fire
but that doesn't give you the right
to be the ones who give him his labels.
Tony is a tattered cover
and sixteen chapters of broken glass
but if you stick with it long enough
you'll see Tony is worth a
place on the bookshelf.
Tony is the old paint.
Tony is the rubble and the wrecking ball.
Tony is the chaos and the calm,
and anybody would be lucky
to have a friend
like Tony.

MINDFRUIT

Humans consist of 60% water
so, does this make me 60% cucumber?
If I had it my way
I'd probably be a fruit
rather than a vegetable.
I'd be a grape. Why? Good question.
Well, grapes have friends
hanging out on their little branches
bad mouthing the pineapple
for his wacky hair.
It's all going well.
Also, whenever I buy grapes,
I never finish them
which makes my chances of survival
much, much higher.
It's all going well.
That is until you watch
your friend orange
get his skin peeled off
and well , then you're mentally scarred.
None of your grape friends
went to college
so a therapist is out of the question
and you're just drowning in trauma.

Then you watch all your other friends
get chopped up into pieces
and thrown into a blender
with their seeds spilling everywhere
it is not pretty.
I didn't dream this idea,
I wrote this when I was sober
and conscious.
I'm a little bit left field.
By a little bit I mean,
I bought some front row tickets
off a guy named Greg on the Internet,
and I'm actually two miles away
from the pitch
sitting behind a pillar.
Don't trust the Internet is not the message
I am trying to convey here
even though I did do it convincingly.
The message i am trying to let loose
is that this is me.
Weird as a fruit bowl in a drug den.
I'm the seagull at the beach party,
I'm the slip and tumble
rough and rumble sort of guy.

Clumsy looks graceful
by comparison.
I'm a master at laughing
at my own jokes
and scaring the mcjeebus
out of everybody.
My mind is literally a party 24/7
and the punch is constantly spiked.
My thoughts have accents
I'm two pennies away
from a full penny
and I know nothing
of the sport
they call keeping your shit together.
I know only how to spill
and hold nothing back.
I know only how to be this.

ROGUE ALLURE

She wears make up like a mask
with lipstick the colour of blood
because it is a pack leader's job
to look dangerous.
She grew up in a house
painted in cigarette smoke
and decorated
with beer bottles.
She was told how beautiful
she wasn't so often,
she started to believe it.
From the outside,
this house
was the prettiest on the street.
All that did was teach her
the wrong lessons.
How beauty is only exterior,
 a smile makes the world silent
and these beliefs changed her eyes

from a clear summer
to a stormy winter.
Her math lessons were
consumed only
of counting change
from beer runs and tobacco stops.
Her report cards became joint tips.
Her parents were anywhere
but actually there.
By high school
she had lost every drop of care.
She cared about nothing
so she took everything.
She learnt good grades were so last year
and that fashion wasn't coming back.
She would say fake love
was better than no love at all.
Another false belief.
She built an army out of rejects
and broken people.

They followed her like a shadow
but it wasn't real.
After she flunked out
those people were gone
and alone felt the most alone
it has ever felt.
Her best friend became a needle.
Men became the knife edge
and she cut herself daily
trying to drag out some feeling.
Her lipstick is all natural now,
they call it nicotine stained red.
She has not one but two children now,
and it comes around full cycle
because on the days when she's conscious,
the only words she chooses to assemble
is hey baby, go get mummy some smokes.

LOVE: THE BASTARD PART ONE

She didn't come knocking,
She came flat foot to the lock.
Hinges hanging and triangle signs,
a giant ass exclamation point
screaming, beware of splinters.

She, the one who traveled oceans
to kiss me. She, the one sings the sadness
to sleep. She, smiley faced and googly
eyed, she knows nothing of subtly.

Stolen shirts and new
sounds on the stereo.
I'm not used to something this upbeat.
I'm not used to this tempo,
I know nothing
of this type of happiness.

Sadsadsad. That is me.
My emotions, the snail
on the concrete
trying to outrun the snow,
my heart the wasp
trapped under the glass
and she, the flat palm
willing to carry me.
She, the firm hand

She, cares not about the danger of stings.
My heart it got her good, irises swollen,
chest barely able to contain the beating,
pulse heavy and palms sweaty.
She, the one trained
in revenge arts.
Now we're both
fuckedfuckedfucked

Too deep in love to change it.
I'm not saying I would,
I'm just saying, I couldn't,
not even if it Liam Neeson
was the negotiator.
So in essence, fucked.
The deadly venom called love,
there is no cure or antidote
even if you want it.
so learn to deal with it.

Grab her by the hips
and start dancing,
The world is an endless ball of string,
it always will be
and there parts that will forever remain
unseen so let's start by understanding
what's right in front of us.

Let's wave our arms around
and kick our legs about.
I'll grab her hips and we'll swing,
We'll just fucking dance
because at least that's a start.

She, the keeper of my heart.
She, the Armour plated,
sword wielding,
bad ass bitch.
She, the lover and the fighter.
She, the changer of worlds,

and Love, you bastard,
thank you, because
I don't know who I am
without you now.

FALSE ALARM

As we bumped onto the tarmac all I felt were sudden jolts of relief. The clouds had snuck through the window and made themselves at home in my mind but still, relief. Thirty thousand feet, eight hours and just me and my thoughts, this was never going to be a fairytale ending. We were on the ground but still waiting, the voices overhead grew in annoyance with their repetitive 'please stay seated till the seat belt light goes off' but patience was wearing thin and you could feel it. The relief was short lived, now all that ran through my head was park the plane, park the plane, park. The. Damn. Plane. I couldn't help but think if I just ate a few less cheeseburgers maybe I could straight dive through the window because hell, the fall damage would be less painful than this. Suddenly, the red light turns to grey and we're off to the races. Number five aka thunder gunbarrel has been training for this the whole summer. Hold popped open, bag in hand, coat slung over his arm, child over his shoulder and he's not slowing down. He looks unstoppable but number three is approaching on the right, captain cocknuts comes barging through on the left, the race is on. I never left the gate, I bide my time, my breathe sticky and thick, too much so to get involved in the riot race. By the time I make it to customs the queue rages for miles. Humans become atoms, atoms become molecules, I can't see colours and the sounds become one drowning static. Slowly we move towards the boothes, there isn't enough room to pace, not enough energy to make a fist or grind my teeth, I need air, air I think, there's no air, I can't breathe. I spiral into a blur; time loses itself inside of me and the next thing I hear is some batman wannabe screaming next. The bag on my back has become an anchor as I drag myself to the booth. The man inside it is a house, built of brick and seemingly unmovable. I force the corner of my mouth upwards with everything I have but his face remains a straight line. I feel the lights dim as I transported to a back office with a spotlight. I'm handcuffed to the table as he rattles off question after question after question after question. I respond with as much enthusiasm as possible but my words are heavy and they plummet towards the ground without a parachute and at this point, I'm just guessing.

After what feels like forever, he takes the gun from
my temple and shoots a hole into my passport before
opening the barrier.
Still barely dragging myself around, I notice the exit sign.
Two heavy metal doors into freedom and summer,
I push hard and it blinds me, the black and white sun
hits my face but I instantly deflect it. Home stretch,
still dragging myself around, dead weight, breath still sticky
then I see her. She is dressed in blue with a ferris wheel smile
and her hair is a river. Her eyes call my name in a voice that
would soothe earthquakes. My feelings suddenly leap off the
couch, put on a suit and develop OCD. They start caring
about order and hair without knots. Suddenly, I can breathe.
She runs to me, leaps into my arms and hugs me. The room explodes into colour, I hear bird songs and the future and then
there's my heart; I hear it whispering to me, kiss her kid, kiss
her good, don't let her get away, this one right here isn't a
false alarm, she's the real deal. I smile at her, a genuine fucking
smile before I kiss her slowly.
As I pull away, I tell her I miss her. My words now
have wings, still smiling I ask, 'are you ready?
'For what' she replies.
'US' I say slowly
'US'.

AUTISM

WITH

A CAPITAL

WTF

Autism has its perks, sure.
For example I get a badge
at the airport
which translates to I'm special
and I don't have to queue.
great!
I can even wave
at the thunder faces
as I breeze passed them,
I mean if you got it, flaunt it!
Some people naturally assume
I'm dangerous,
the badge literally screams
mentally unstable
like I could snap at any minute
so I throw out a growl
every now and then
just so they know what's up.
The articles also tell me
my brain has advantages.
My brain can't figure out
what that means but
I always was
the first to find wally
so again... great.

I also have great attention to detail,
I'm a sketch artists wet dream,
a needle in a haystack to me
Is less impossible
because I think outside of the box.
I'm still in a box but my box
is painted in rainbow colours
and smells like fresh cotton sheets
constantly.
This box has a unicorn called Clobselot
and he wears socks even during a heatwave.
Clobselot went skiing
and he didn't bring me back a souvenir,
that was a tough day in my box.
Basically, I have imagination for days.
Everything is more vivid
with autism, lights are more, lighty I guess.
A bright flash, a soft touch, a loud noise
it all burns. Eye contact is like staring
at the sun from a metre away.
My brain is just kindling
searching for a spark.
I don't get Sunday mornings in my mind,
all I get is city rush hour traffic.

Every social occasion
is the equivalent of me bringing a frying
pan
to a gun fight and if I'm lucky
I'll survive the first bullet.
Everything I do is #awkward.
Awkward hugs and awkward smiles,
awkward get me the fuck out of here eyes,
I have always felt too awkward
to ask for anything
so I've just made do.
I learnt to love myself... Great.
I learnt independence... Great.
Then I spent so much time trying to fit in,
I found myself more lost than I've ever
been.
Autism isn't all coffee and donuts
but it could sure as hell be a lot worse.
Without autism I wouldn't be here
writing this.
Without autism I wouldn't be who I am
and I wouldn't change that for the world.

Sure autism makes you a little different
but what two people are the same?
Find your quirks and embrace them.
Love how the grass feels
the day after it's rained.
Try and learn
the language of the wind.
You don't have to be autistic
to appreciate the little things.
Autism taught me
it's okay to be weird,
Its okay to be afraid,
it taught me how we're all human
and we're all wired differently.
Autism
you monster trucker,
you're freaking awesome.

SOLO

Let it break down, let rain come
and leak through the sunroof.
Let the wheels fly off
and let's tell the universe
to take its best shot.
Let's get back up,
brush off the anchors
and smile.
There will always be times
where we fall
and get knocked down
by the weight of this world.
Times where some magical force
shatters the calm we have built.
However, believe me when I say
never will I not be here
to help put the pieces back together.
Alone is gone now
and I'm sorry,
but it's never coming back again.

There is no me
without you
anymore.
I am the bumble
and you, the bee.
I, the rain storm
and you the sunshine.
The rainbow, our love,
the meet in the middle,
the colour combating
the grey.
There is no me
without you
anymore.

BLACK AND YELLOW

S
N
O
W

Hey snow,
you sexy little substance.
I love the way you fall fast,
spreading yourself out
just white and.... naked.
Snow,
I love it when you tickle my neck,
I just want to feel you in my hands,
hell, I'll even take my gloves off
and watch as you melt away!
Snow, I want to lay down
and feel every inch of you.
Snow, why can't you freeze time
so it can be me and you forever?
I have felt this way
since I first saw you,
it was love at first sight
and snow, I know
you're not in town often
but why
can't you settle
for me?

we are
the bandits
dripping
in bravery

D
R
I
V
E

Give me darkness with a half moon in the distance and let try and catch it. Give me a car that runs with a radio loud enough to drown out the noise in my mind.Give me Springsteen or Seger. Bad Company or Boston and you can watch as the weight lifts. I am a man plagued with too much thought in too little head and I drown daily in what ifs. My worst enemy is me and I am great at creating boundaries .I am capable but I doubt I will ever truly believe it. Give me a road and let's see where I go. Not even I know where I am heading but my heart is telling me to leave. So, give me the wheel and a place far enough to escape anything familiar. Give the songs time to absorb into my skin and sink into my soul. Let the calm wash over me as I push it to 90. I just want a millimoment, a fraction of a second to know how it feels, how it really feels to be free.

It is the unknown that strikes the hardest.
It is the sadness drenched in stealth
and submission holds.
I am a question mark stretched so far
I have become an exclamation point.
I am rage in a bottle, smashed
on a bar edge
and held up to the throat of sanity.
I am answerless.
I do not know why sadness has come
but it is here and it is way too comfortable
to leave.

S
O
S

TEXAS

In Texas
there are only two seasons.
Summer and holy shit SUMMER.
The only difference between hell
and Texas, is air conditioning.

Gosh darn it, humidity
is a bitch, right Texas?
You would know.

In Texas
there's a taco stand on every corner
and the Texan equivalent to oxygen
is brisket.

In Texas
BBQ sauce is the solution
to every problem ever!
Fall down and graze your knee?
Rub BBQ sauce on it!
Burnt your toast? Put BBQ sauce
on it!

In Texas.
People drive like they're trying to outrun
a storm
and think highway rules are for suckers.
In Texas, fender benders
are a sport event and if this was the
Olympics,
Texas would win gold.

Texas,
you are 790 miles of instant sunburn.
A vampires worst nightmare
but Texas,
you are the lone star
I haven't convinced myself
is a satellite yet.

LOVE: THE BASTARD

PART TWO

And when she leaves you,
the love within you will not.
The venom will manifest itself
into a parasite and it will
start talking to you.

You will stop combing your hair.
You will stop buying
clothes that fit you
and you will convince yourself
it is enough.
You will buy a suitcase and fill it
with a million bad ideas,
you will become a salesman,
giving pieces of yourself
away for pennies
and you will forget who you are.
You will stop speaking in bird songs
and become fluent in silence.

You will lock yourself away
and make art
using only fists and dry wall.

and the love within you
will transform itself into hatred.
You will sword fight with middle fingers
and your tongue will become a revolver.
You will not stop shooting,
and then you will turn the barrel
on yourself
because nothing can hurt you
more than your own thoughts
But it's toolatetoolatetoolate.

She, will still be beautiful.
She, will always be the saviour.
And you will believe
she, will be the only one
who will ever make you smile.
You will believe there is nobody else,
you will remember
all the other fish in the sea
but you don't want a fish,
you want a bad ass
mother fucking mermaid.

God damn it, it's so
Fuckedfuckedfucked.

Because even though it was poison,
you ordered seconds.
You sipped it like
cheap champagne
and convinced yourself
it is was melted gold
overandover
until you believed it.

She, will move on.
She will be happy
and then you
will make more art.
Only this time
you will use razor blades and skin.
You will open bottle after bottle
just trying to find
a version of yourself
that you don't hate.
You will start living in stumbles,

drowning the last remaining
pieces of you
and then you will fall,
you will look up
at the sky
and you will mumble,

Love, you bastard, fuck you.
I don't know who I am
with you anymore.

B
O
X

I'm not saying
I want to put you
in a box but
if somebody
gave me a box
and you
just so happened
to be inside it,
it would instantly
become
my favourite
box.

There are days I wake up
and I am miles away
from anywhere.
My first order of business
is convincing my eye lids
to stay open.
I lost count of the mornings
where I have to wrestle
my own body out of bedsheets.
I have lost count
of the times I have lost.
The times
where the duvet
becomes the lid
to the coffin,
the times
I must to beg my mind
to let me rest in peace.
I have been a lead weight
in a sea of self-doubt,

OPINIONS

I have hated myself
more than you ever could,
so don't tell me you understand
and don't blame me
if I don't care
what you think of me.

When sadness
comes knocking,
let it in.
Cook it
its favourite meal,
get it drunk,
make it spill
its secrets
then toss it
in a cab
and send
it home.

FARE

WHEN I SAY I

When I say I love you
what I'm really saying
is that you're so beautiful
I can't breathe!
If it was you vs oxygen

....

you'd always win.

LOVE YOU PART 1

When a bird came
barreling out of the sky
and collided
with my kitchen window,
I scooped him up
off the ground
with my bear paws
and nursed him back
to health.
I didn't put him in a cage,
I placed him on the counter top
and fed him seeds from my fingers.
As he sipped water
from an egg cup,
I saw the life slowly return
to his eyes.
Eventually, he perched himself
on my finger
and I saw hope claw its way
back into his body
and claim victory again.
He chirped out a thank you,
I told him,
you're welcome
and this is an example
of just how easy
kindness can be.

FEATHERS

SOMETIMES

THE

DARKNESS

SINGS

SOMETIMES

I

HUM

ALONG

BONE SHAKER

When I'm gone
and there's no bones
left to shake,
where will the excitement go?
I think I'm okay with being a ghost.
No sleep deprivation,
no please, leave me alone,
no checking I locked the door
for the millionth time
and I imagine
when I want to be gone
I can just go.
It might take a while to adjust,
I imagine ghost powers
take a little getting used to
but before long
I'll be doing all sorts
of ghostly things
like turning off lights
and moving books slightly.

Maybe ghosts even have
ghost burgers with ghost cheese
and ghost bacon
and hopefully not ghost attacks.
Like heart attacks but more ghosty.
Maybe ghosts have the best
educational system
and I could land myself
a sweet ghost job
scaring the eeby jeebs
out of unwanted residents.
Like a realtor but better.
I would take the master class
in ghost University and
eventually, I'd ace it.
Sure, I'd flunk a few times
but what's the rush
I'm already dead.
In the meantime, I'd take a job

in a mail room
and make some ghost buddies
and we'd goof around
and send mail to the humans
to really freak them out.
That is of course
if there isn't a gap
in the market for ghost poetry
but I'd be battling with the greats
and I'd really have to step my game up.
On the other hand, If I couldn't afford
rent for my ghost apartment
I'd just walk through the walls
and live anywhere I wanted.
Sure you wouldn't be there
and that would suck but
maybe I could learn
to haunt you
lovingly.
I'm sure even ghosts
have their off days
but I don't think their off
is as off as this off
and look human I'm sorry,

I will find a way to pay for that lamp.

I'm sorry death, you just don't scare me.
Fear doesn't vibrate these bones
only joy knows how to shake them.
I'm a make the most of it sort of man.
Throw me in a crocodile pit
and I will emerge a few fingers short
with the title Crocodile King.
I became such good friends with words
they don't have the heart
to hurt me anymore,
and when I say I'm invisible,
this is exactly what I mean.

Smile
like it makes
sense
and maybe,
one day
it will

I am at war
with the devil
and the taxi man.
Destination unknown
but there's a ten
in my wallet
so push the gas
and start the meter.
Go give it all you got
and get me somewhere
close to home.
The engine churns
and we swing a left.

The seafront
is cluttered
with overcrowded bars
and theatre girls
who are already
on their second act.
They are zig zag
bullet dodgers
but tonight
I do not hold
the gun.

An unwelcome whisper
fills my ear
and advises
I get possessed
by the party
because what's one shot
or six
if you've already
lost your mind?

My view unchanged

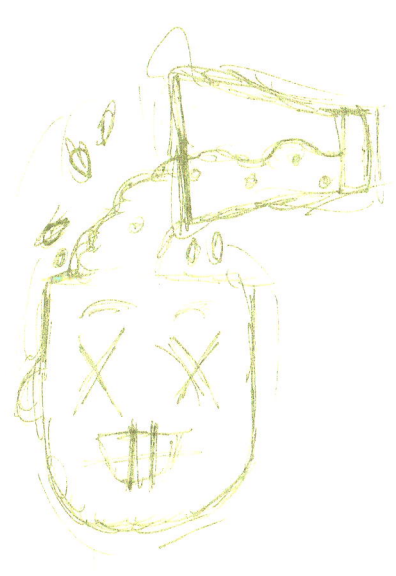

I collapse into the backseat
eyes closed as I feel
this metal shell
throw us down
as endless string
of streets.
My brain
collides with
my skull
like a penny
in a jar
well shaken.

I sold my soul
to a taxi driver
to be alone
with my thoughts
in a reckless attempt
to try and escape you.

My demon, my love,
eyes open now.
The meter flashing nine,
we're almost out of time,
we are almost,
out of time.

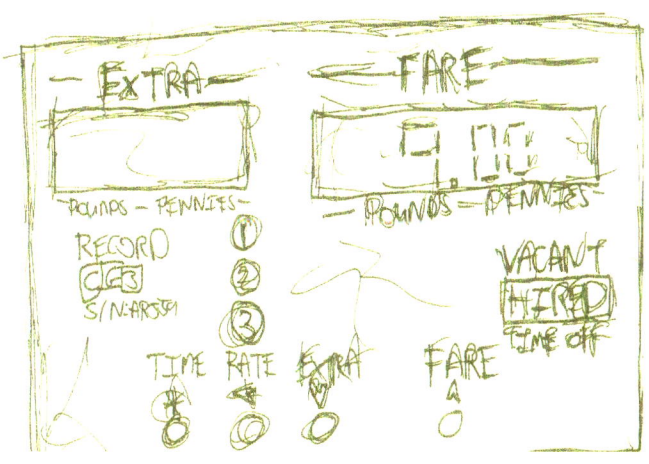

ROLLERCOASTERS

Just last night,
we laughed each other to sleep,
talking nonsense
and joking like a couple vets
who'd by skin and teeth
made it out of the trenches.
Fuck, that was a winter of bloodshed,
that was a winter where I took
my fair share of fist shaped bullets
for you and all you could say was
'Why! Why won't you leave me alone?'
You told me your seasons
aren't weather determined.
Your summer is a smile
and a frantic want
to be anything but still
and your downs are your winters.
This was the third ice age
in a few years but here you are,
a survivor still.

Just last night,
you told me

how it was going to be okay.
How the future
was an open road,
how you had
 an endless tank
and you didn't know
where you were going
but the best part
of the journey
is figuring it out.

I woke this morning
to the sound of you crying.
Tears frozen before they fell,
winter again.
There is not a second
you are safe from the shifting.
The weatherman predicted
clear skies but here we are
soaked through and freezing.
Global warming is here,
the summers are getting shorter
and the pollution
from bad thoughts is on the rise.

All I want to do,
is swipe away the grey clouds,
put your storms in a box
and burn it.
All I want is sunshine
stubborn enough to stay
forever,
all I want to do
is punch your pain
in its stupid face
and tell it to leave town
and to never come back.

Just last night you told me
how sadness would one day
become a distant memory.
How the seasons would steady
and how the fighting would go to bed.
Now all I have left to ask,
is what are we waiting for?
Isn't it about time,
we make that a reality.

Authenticity,
a fashion that's fading.
Never will I succumb
to be anything but this.
Never will I squeeze
into a mould
I was never designed
to fit into.
I will not change
for the sake
of being loved,
or lose
who I am
for material gain.
I am me
and that is all
I will ever be.

A
U
T
H
E
N
T
I
C

UNBORN

When you join us, join us open minded.
Join us when we're on the brink
of a breakdown and restore all hope.
Join us whenever you feel ready,
and attempt to brace yourself
but be warned, you can't prepare
for how much love
I got stored away for you.
I'm going to strap you to my chest
and we're going become both sides
of a Velcro arrangement.
(Get used to those sorts of phrases,
I make stupid comparisons A LOT)
I'm going to teach you
all I know, starting with home.
Home is the right arms cradling you,
peace, peace is the heartbeat
overdosed on love and love,
love is that feeling of the last click
of a million-piece puzzle inside you.
I will raise you on dumb jokes,
poetry and rock music.
I will write you a poem everyday
and read it to you before bedtime.
I will teach you how to play sports really
badly
and prove to you that not all ideas are good.

I will teach you how to laugh after a bad fall
and show you there's nothing
a little love can't fix.
Also, don't tell mum
but we're gonna overnap
like champions!
Before you get here though,
I got to warn you
of a few more things.
You're going to meet a lot of people very
quickly.
They're going to talk to you in weird voices
and pull ridiculous faces at you.
I'm sorry kid but you're on your own for this
one,
I can't help, you're just going to
have to power through it but I believe in you.
There will also come a lot of unexpected,
but luckily I have a knack for weathering
storms.
There is so much you have to learn
and I am going to be there every step of the
way.
Join us when you feel like it,
we'll be ready.
And together we can all truly learn
the definition of happiness.

Let us tangle
and twist
into one
another.
Didn't you
know,
this
is how
storms
are born

What if we were always
destined to wind up here?
Imagine there were
no other roads
that lead to us.
What if we had to go there
to get where we are.
What if we had to endure
all that pain
to find one another.
What if our mistakes
brought us here.
Would you believe
your wrongs
were rights
all along?

THE

ROAD

THE AGE

The world is on fire but it's fine.
The detective, apocalypse
has almost solved this case
but like I said, it's fine.
We are the tip toer generation
unaware that the ice age
we all fear
is already upon us.
These days we walk
on thin sheets of ice,
there are winter winds
within our screens
and the keyboard warriors
roam those streets.
It's just hatred
all the way down.
Kindness is the smaller needle
in a stack of needles.
Kindness is the Loch ness
monster sighting
everybody labels
a hoax.

Happiness these days
is constructed
from the ashes
of yesterday.
Yes, idiots do
rule the world
and yes,
it is scary
but it's fine.
Instead of stressing
let's start smiling.
Lets make the most
of what we have,
kick up a chair,
put marshmallows on a stick
and let's laugh about the
good ole times.
This world is a bonfire,
so, let's just enjoy it
before it's all gone.

WHEN I SAY I

Okay, when I say I love,
what I'm really saying
is I don't know
what it means
but it means
everything.
Love is the curiosity
that will one day kill me
and I'm so lost in it
right now,
build the coffin,
arrange the flowers,
bring on my burial.

LOVE YOU PART 2

I expected a million sunsets
over a million beaches as the
birds sang a million lullabies.
Suddenly rainbows. The high five that
landed perfect and woke the dead. Turns
out my aim was off. I missed the hand and
met the face. No rainbows, just rain. Puddles
and an exhausted sun giving an unenthused
thumbs up. Flashbacks to guitar lessons.
Wrong string, wrong chord,
wrong everything.
Flashbacks to the teacher yelling 'YOU'RE
DOING IT WRONG'. Like ice skating but
with lips and no barrier. My first time in
the water but nobody around to save
me. No armbands. No goggles. No safety.
Nearly drowned, barely made it out.
So tell me, why am I so eager to swim again?

FIRST KISS

STILLNESS

Too often distracted
by God knows what.

Just distracted.

The tip tap on the window,
maybe.

The first rain drop of downpour,
I heard it,
maybe.

I guess it's the nothing,
the everything and all
that rests in between.

Just distracted.

I've never been stillness.
All I know is motion

and gas pedals
on ground floors.

All I know is the spin
and the stumble.
I know nothing of
straight lines
or one way roads.

I know all about playing dead
to the grizzly bear
named Monday.

Is there correlation,
I don't know,
maybe.

I just got distracted.

THE CLASSIC

Let me
buy you dinner.
I'll pull out your chair,
and we will chit chat
about the nothings
and everything's of life.
Let me
walk you home,
and as we approach
the front door,
I'll stand waiting for that
one
awkward
moment
where we
could possibly
fall
dangerously
in
love.

Depression is not the ghost,
it is the haunted house
that refuses to occupy
logical reason.

Depression is the winter
that overstayed its welcome,
it has been here so long
I don't remember
how summer actually feels.

Depression is the layer
upon layer
hiding the real me from the
world.
My shadow is a stranger,
my mirrors
close their eyes
every time I enter the room
and my windows
are still waiting
for the show to start.

NUCLEAR

Depression doesn't come
with an instruction manual
but if it did,
it would be written
in a language
you can only read
when you've lost
all hope.

If you understand this,
I'm sorry.

When getting dressed
is the mountain climb
in terrestrial downpour.
Where finding a pair of socks
is a life or death situation.
This is a feeling,
I never want you to understand,
because if you understand
that means you once went there,
it means you wore the t shirt
even on the days you
wanted to be nothing
but skin.

Depression is the destination
red striked and ridden
with radioactive signs.
Please, I am begging you,
turn the car around,
take your smile
and go back home.
Erase this place from your maps
because this is a place
I never want you
to get to.

LOVE: THE BASTARD

PART THREE

And a day will come
where you will wake up
and you will suddenly
have the strength
to peel yourself
off the wall
of sadness.

You will still love her
but it will no longer hurt
to love her. The wound
will heal but the scar
will forever remain.

However,
it will not resemble
pain, it will resemble
a war you survived through.
The movie you have been directing
will be cancelled
and you will return to reality
and start seeing everything
for what it truly is.

You will return to the art form
called sunshineandsmiles.
Colour will creep in
and conquer the grey.
You will stop abusing the digits
on the microwave and seek
apologises from the stove top.
You will no longer fear mirrors
and you will once again
start singing your favourite
songs in the shower.

You will relearn self-care
and remember the joy
you found in the little things.
You will step outside,
the sun will no longer
burn your skin
and you will smile,
a genuine fucking smile.

And eventually
you will move on
and fuckfuckfuck,

it will feel so
god damn good.

You will laugh
and out loud
you will mumble.

Love, you complicated
bastard,
I love you.

I fear one day I will stop being
the right train at the right station taking
you exactly where you need to be and
instead I will become the delayed flight home.
I will be lost baggage you no longer search
for and I will be the turbulence you can't
handle anymore.
I am a composition of rough landings
and storms that stop the take off.
The engine that struggles to start more as
time ticks away! I fear I will never
be good enough for forever.
That I will one day become the house plant
you forget to water.

However, I am working on self-belief.
Today,
I looked in the mirror
winked at myself and asked myself
if I've been working out lately.
Tomorrow, I'm going to ask myself
on a date and we're gonna go get
coffee and self-sabotage will not be invited.

Things are starting to look up
and you, are the reason for it all.

S
E
L
F

L
O
V
E

RAINBOW

Those colourful beauties
that follow the rainfall,
the unicorn slides,
the paths to gold,
rainbows,
putting colour
into the grey
since like
forever ago!
I know I shouldn't trust
anything
that has been that happy
for that long but,
rainbows!
Rainbows don't have bad days
but they always have the blues
so maybe that's the secret.
That joke was stupid
but maybe rainbows
like bad jokes.

The secret could just be
love yourself.
Love all of your colours
and don't beat yourself up
for having quirks.

The rainbow represents
all the colours
of all emotions all at once
and loves every shade of itself.
The rainbow gives rain the
middle finger and says
- you can't crash this party!

So on the days with clouds
and without hope
look upwards
and remember this.
Whatever it is,
you can do it.
You can, you can, you can
be the rainbow

WEATHERED

A small rock hitting glass is a familiar sound. It's a slight ding, a vibration small enough to shake cobwebs and unsettle the spiders that rest in them. Some flies may even break free. At 3:33 that ding becomes a thud, a thunder strike that moves every atom of you and the sleeping bricks shake suddenly out of slumber. Silence holds its breathe, pipes become nervous and creak. There it is again. The ding now an explosion that echoes down hallways and scratches its claws on your door. You close your eyes and ignore it. The small rock isn't a rock anymore. It's everything but. It's the ghost you never noticed, it's the intruders footsteps, something is lurking. As you creep out of bed you are now a siren. Your sledgehammer legs slam on the wood. The door gains a hundred pounds as you pry it open with all your might. Peeking, checking the coast is clear you step out. The shuffle of bricks from the thunderclaps has caused the hallways to triple in length. You creep. Legs, sledgehammers still, you hear it. A pitter patter on full volume, it's deafening. Inhale. Inhale. Inhale. Breathe out. You push against the fear, the door flings open and you see the sound. The hailstorm. The rain rocks rapping on the window but you don't notice the sound anymore. All you can see, all you can focus on, is the streetlight reflection of you framed in the night. The rain on the window showing how many pieces of you remain. You are broken. You are a shattered story and you know, the only visitor that has come is the grief, you refuse to shake.

Wake up
and shake me
with that
look
that screams,
today,
you are
mine!

LOVE DRUNKK

When I look back now,
I don't remember the beginning
very clearly.
I didn't drink when I met you
but I was drunk off something.
I must have drank a bottle
or a shot or something
because through the haze
all I see is that smile.
I remember sentences
wrestling themselves
back into my mouth
and letters
tripping over one another.
I remember my brain being on
fire
and trying to extinguish it
with gasoline.
I don't remember the first words
you said
but I know they
were a rose garden.

There are gaps in my memory,
Pivotal moments I took photos
of
with shaky hands
but through the blur
I know happiness is alive
and partying like a freshman
who just got his student loan.
And I know you've told me
a thousand times
but I don't know what made
you love me.
However,
whatever it was,
whatever we did,
it got us here
and I would never
want to change that.

MINUS LIFE

Depression is a magnet.
Depressive people
have depressive friends
but we still don't get it.
I once told a friend to toughen up
because he said
he was too sad to move.
This was before I knew
depressions name,
before I saw it in the mirror,
before it followed me disguised
as a shadow
and whispered in my ear
but even now
my depression is different.
On most days it's an
obstacle I feel I can over come,
it's a weight
I've grown used to carrying
but to some
that obstacle is too high.
That weight is an anchor
and that metaphor works two ways.

It's either dragging you down
or keeping you in the port of sadness
and stopping you from going out to sea
and finding your way home!
I wonder
if I listened more
to the words he wasn't saying,
did more than pat him on the shoulder
and tell him it's okay when it wasn't,
if I took the time to listen,
toughened up myself
and just told him
you will not be defeated,
depression does not define you,
you can beat this!
I wonder then,
I wonder if he'd still be alive

WHEN I SAY I

When I say I love you,
what I'm really trying to say is,
thank you.
Thank you for turning this mind noise
from deafening static
to a sunny Sunday morning
in the countryside.
Thank you
for shining bright
even when the world
turns its lights off.
I don't want to sound cheesy but,
when you kiss me
I forget what words are.
I scrap more love poems than I keep
because none of them feel good enough
anymore.
You make me believe that heaven
is just ancient slang
for being in love.
Thank you,

LOVE YOU PART 3

for rolling your eyes
every time I do something dumb

and letting me know it's stupid.
I'm also sorry,
you must have really sore eyes.
I find myself out of sorts these days.
I caught myself the other day
listening to pop songs
and understanding them.
What have you done to me.
But anyway,
still, thank you.
Thank you
for being the beachball
in a sea of white flags
and trust me when I say,
I'm going to love you forever
the exact way
I ice skate.
Dangerously,
with no idea
how to stop.

You are the
ripple
on the water
whispering
to the wave
and teaching it
of stillness

THE FANTASY FACTORY

Is where I go
when I run out of reality
to hide behind.

The door is old wood embedded
into even older tree.

There's a sign just outside that says,
no reality allowed.
Leave your troubles
with the fairies,
they aren't welcome in
here.

The door opens upwards,
it reveals a stairwell
made completely out of
the residue of rainbows.
I mean,
have you ever?

Down the stairs
there are coat hooks
for your serious
and pouches
for your gravity.

138

You float and bounce
in the fantasy factory,
there's no walking required.

The unicorn express isn't compulsory
but it is recommended
and it runs every second.

The factory belts are sugar coated
and taste like strawberries.
The furniture is comprised
of nothing but candy floss
and a little bit of elf magic.
You can eat all you can dream
at the fantasy factory,
there aren't no calories there.

The factory is everything
you have ever wanted,
the relaxation and
the come alive.
There is no night at the factory,
unless you want it to be
typically there's
only the sun slung snuggly
on a hammock in the sky
whistling with the birds.

See we made a deal here,
not too much heat,
just enough
and you can stay, forever.
The moon comes by
every now and then
just to soak in the blue,
he sets up a couple deck chairs
and the sun and the moon
sit and sip some sky
whilst sharing stories
about the stars.

The fantasy factory
is the vacation
for everyday,
and I know you haven't
heard of it but
the fantasy factory is real
because the fantasy factory
is just new slang
for imagination.

It may be
the end

but in no
way is it
over

(SILENCE)

ACKNOWLEDGEMENTS

There honestly isn't enough paper in this world to contain the gratitude I'd like to express. There are too many people to thank and honestly, I'd probably fumble it with my rambling. So let me leave this short and let me leaave this sweet.

Hey YOU, yes you! Reader, supporter, friend, human, alien and everything in between. Thank You. Without you this book, this crazy dream, the chasing, the fighting, none of it would be possible.

Mind Noise is only the beginning and some day down the road, I will see you all and we're going to hug and it's going to be awkward and it is going to be beautiful. The support means the world to me,

until next time,

your friendly neighbourhood poet

Ash Raymond James

ABOUT THE AUTHOR

Ash Raymond James is a writer from
South Wales, UK.
He is also one half of Red Kite Collective,
a graphic design and photography business ran
with his partner Savanna Rose Phibbs.
Find the business @wearedkite
and wearedkite.com

If you are looking for Ash, find him
@ashraymondjames on all the social media
sites including Spotify, Youtube, Instagram and on
Patreon where he has runs an
exclusive poetry community.

www.ashraymondjames.com
www.patreon.com/ashraymondjames

Made in the USA
Coppell, TX
10 September 2020